First published in Great Britain in 2022 by Farshore,
An imprint of HarperCollins*Publishers*
1 London Bridge Street, London SE1 9GF
www.farshore.co.uk

HarperCollins*Publishers*
1st floor, Watermarque Building, Ringsend Road
Dublin 4, Ireland

Written by Thomas McBrien
Special thanks to Sherin Kwan, Alex Wiltshire and Milo Bengtsson

This book is an original creation by Farshore.

ISBN 978 0 0084 9598 5
3
Printed in Spain

ONLINE SAFETY FOR YOUNGER FANS

Spending time online is great fun! Here are a few simple rules to help younger fans stay safe and keep the internet a great place to spend time:
- Never give out your real name – don't use it as your username.
- Never give out any of your personal details.
- Never tell anybody which school you go to or how old you are.
- Never tell anybody your password except a parent or a guardian.
- Be aware that you must be 13 or over to create an account on many sites.
Always check the site policy and ask a parent or guardian for permission before registering.
- Always tell a parent or guardian if something is worrying you.

Stay safe online. Any website addresses listed in this book are correct at the time of going to print. However, Farshore is not responsible for content hosted by third parties. Please be aware that online content can be subject to change and websites can contain content that is unsuitable for children. We advise that all children are supervised when using the internet.

MIX
Paper from responsible sources
FSC™ C007454

This book is produced from independently certified FSC™ paper to ensure responsible forest management.

For more information visit: www.harpercollins.co.uk/green

MINECRAFT

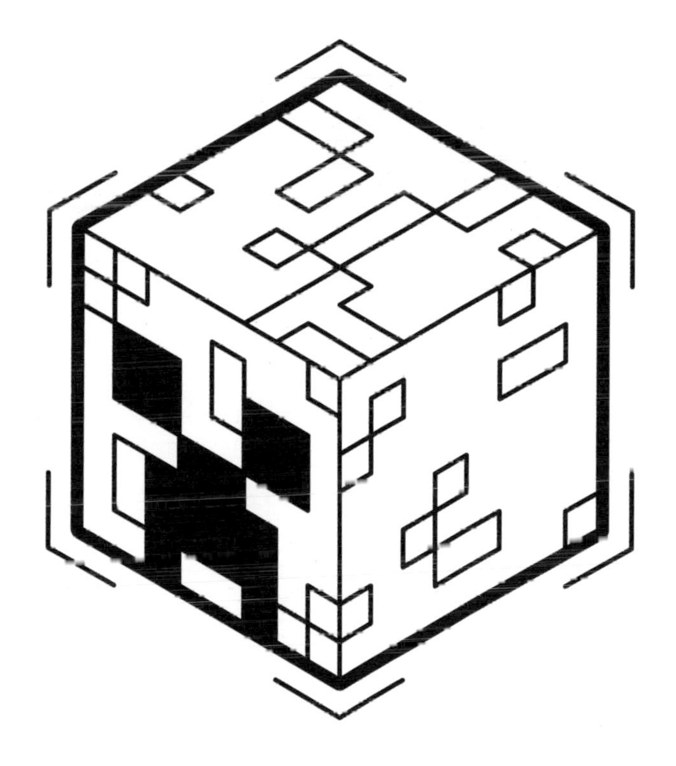

ANNUAL
2023

MOJ
ANG
STUDIOS

CONTENTS

15 29 56

HELLO!

Welcome to the Minecraft Annual 2023! It's good to take a moment with you to look over all we've been doing in Minecraft for the past year.

Let's see, we've splashed through mangrove swamps. We've tip-toed through ancient subterranean cities. We've politely asked allays to collect all that cobblestone we left lying around while mining. We've run away – very quietly – from terrifying wardens. In short, it's been a busy year!

On the pages to come, we'll explore what else has been going on in and around Minecraft, such as the work of Block by Block. This foundation, which is run by Mojang and the United Nations, uses Minecraft to help build better cities. Pretty inspirational, right? We'll visit Sao Paulo in Brazil to see one of its projects.

Back at the studio, some of our team will tell you about their favourite features that we've added to Minecraft over the past few updates. We've also created guides to making your very own mob (what horrors and delights will you make?!) and using the super-powerful command block (can you handle the POWER?).

We've also ventured out into the Overworld. Can you brave the elements (and heights) when you take on the challenge of surviving at the top of a mountain? Can you build an amazing base at the bottom of the ocean?

And there's lots more besides. We hope you've enjoyed your year in Minecraft as much as we have. We love having you along with us on our adventure!

Alex Wiltshire
MOJANG STUDIOS

A YEAR IN MINECRAFT

EXPERT GUIDE WITH SPARKS

It's been another exciting year in the world of Minecraft, with bigger caves, cuter mobs and an ever-growing community. It seems as though there's a new announcement every few weeks, whether it's new updates and events, or new platforms and crossovers being announced. Let's take a tour of some of the biggest highlights from the last year.

MINECRAFT LIVE

Lydia Winters and the Mojang crew hosted Minecraft Live and showcased all the latest updates coming to the Minecraft universe this year.

CROCO ISLAND

Mojang teamed up with Lacoste to not only bring out an awesome fashion range, but also a brand-new map, which can be explored in Bedrock Edition, called Croco Island. Grab your friends and head down to the tennis courts, compete in mini-games, enjoy scavenger hunts and parkour courses, and meet the island's toothy inhabitant – a giant crocodile!

BEDROCK & JAVA PARITY

Want to share that perfect Bedrock seed with your Java friends? Now you can! With Bedrock and Java parity, the worlds are now more identical than ever.

AXOLOT' OF FUN

The cute axolotl has joined the team. These aquatic companion mobs will help you battle the drowned and heal you when you need it.

DEFEAT OF THE VENGEFUL HEART OF ENDER

Minecraft Dungeons players reached the end of the Orb of Dominance saga with the defeat of the Vengeful Heart of Ender in the Echoing Void DLC.

THE WILD UPDATE

The next major update was brought out: The Wild Update! Discover its scary new adventures and beautiful new landscapes.

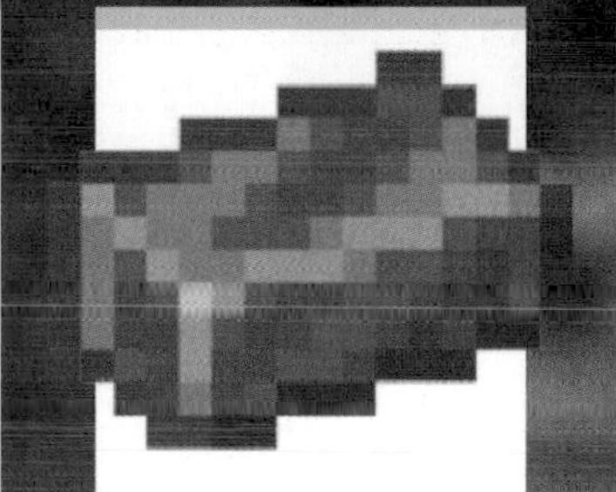

NEW METAL

Miners are on the lookout for a new ore as they go digging underground – copper!

GAME PASS FOR PC

Say hello to the ever-growing Minecraft community with the addition of both Minecraft: Bedrock Edition and Minecraft: Java Edition to the Xbox PC Game Pass.

MINECRAFT RTX

Players got to experience Minecraft in a whole new light using Nvidia's real-time ray-tracing software, transforming the blocky universe into a smooth new playground.

DISNEY MEETS MINECRAFT

It's time to play a visit to Walt Disney World! For their 50th anniversary, Disney is working with Mojang to bring our favourite characters and video game together on one screen.

MINECRAFT LIVE

Were you among the millions of players who watched as all the upcoming updates were announced to the Minecraft community? Those who tuned in live were the first to hear what's in store for Minecraft over the next 12 months, from the newest and cutest new mobs to the unveiling of the next big update to come. Let's look at what was announced here.

CAVE GENERATION

The long-anticipated overhaul of Minecraft's underground caves has arrived with bigger caves, deeper caverns and massive underwater ravines. This is one of the biggest changes to happen since the Overworld popped into existence. Big shout-out to the players who tested it!

OLD & NEW

A collective sigh of relief was audible, as it was confirmed that existing worlds will safely merge with the Caves & Cliffs Update Part II. That's right! Updating your world to the latest version will keep your builds safe, with new caves generating around your current game.

MOB VOTE

It was a close vote, with players battling through three rounds to pick their favourite new mob to join the Minecraft landscape. The winner by popular demand was the allay! The allay is a flying mob that searches for items and brings them to you. CUTE! Have you met one yet?

MINECRAFT THE WILD UPDATE

THE WILD UPDATE

Hear ye, hear ye! The latest update was announced! Have you been enjoying the beautiful nature and scary adventures In the Wild Update? If not, what are you waiting for? It features derpy frog variants, a scary new hostile mob and some exciting new biomes for you to explore.

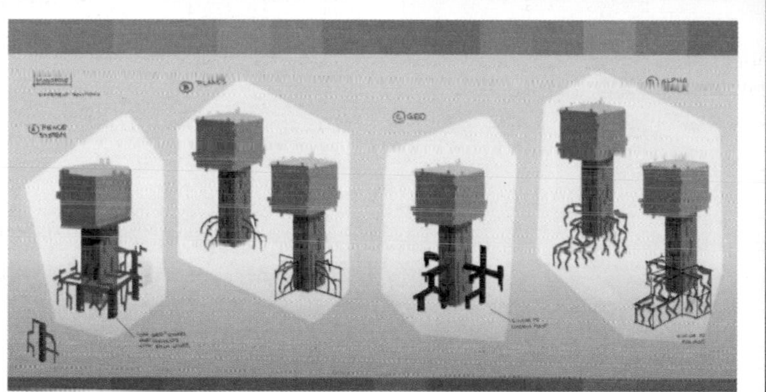

MANGROVE SWAMP BIOME

There's a new swamp biome in the Overworld! We love the new water-resistant trees, mangroves, with their large, visible roots. These are the first saplings that can be planted underwater.

THE DEEP DARK

Viewers got their first good look at the deep dark, which has turned out to be just as scary as it seemed! You need to move very quietly to avoid awakening the warden, deep dark's fierce new mob. They are blind, so they rely on smell and vibrations to find you.

FROGS

The most ribbiting mob to date – frogs! Frogs jump around on lily pads and dripleaves, and lay tadpoles in swamps. Just like in nature, frogs will have different variants depending on where they grow up. Snowy frogs are raised in cold biomes and tropical frogs in warm biomes.

SURVIVAL CHALLENGE
FROZEN PEAKS

Fight for survival in one of the newest and coolest biomes – a frozen peak! Surviving in this cold landscape will pit you against new challenges – jagged cliffs, powder snow, strays ... even the goats can be a menace. Complete each of these steps and see if you can survive atop one of Minecraft's tallest mountain peaks.

1 MOUNTAINEERING

Pack the snowy mountain climbing essentials! To reach the tops of peaks safely, you should have a spyglass, leather boots and climbing blocks such as ladders or scaffolding. The boots are important – they'll keep you from falling into dangerous powder snow.

2 HERMIT LIFE

Prepare for your life atop a mountain. Resources can be scarce, so grab some wool to make a bed (and for keeping warm) and other useful blocks, like wood for tools and food for eating.

3 I SPY

It's time to find a frozen peak. Grab your bags and head out in one direction with your spyglass in hand. Use the spyglass to check the tops of peaks for snow as you pass – you're looking for the tell-tale sign of blue packed ice. When it gets dark, use the bed to sleep and stay safe from mobs.

4 CLIMB

Once you find a frozen peak, get climbing! Remember to put on those leather boots. Keep climbing until you reach the top. Watch out for goats – you don't want to be knocked back down to the base of the mountain.

5 BARRIERS

Frozen peaks are covered with ice and packed ice, making it very slippery. Place fences around any jagged cliff edges so you don't fall to an untimely end when sliding across the ice.

6 HOME SWEET HOME

When you reach the top, build a small hut to store your bed and supplies. Place some torches or campfires to light up the area around you – this will melt the snow and stop mobs from spawning in your new home.

SURVIVAL CHALLENGE
FROZEN PEAKS

PART 3

7 SLAYING FOR SEEDS

Next, it's time to ensure you have a supply of food. Grab a sword and slay some skeletons – you're looking to find some bones. Once you have bones, craft bone meal and look for some dirt blocks at the base of the mountain to put down at the peak. Use the bone meal to grow grass, then chop it down to loot wheat seeds.

8 ICE IS FROZEN WATER

You'll need to create some farmland, and for this you'll need water. Find two ice blocks and break them with a pickaxe to create a water source. Then use a bucket to create an infinite water source by placing two water sources two blocks apart.

10 MINING EXPEDITION

Now that you're all set up to survive, it's time to build. Before you can build though, you're going to need some blocks! Dig a mineshaft into the mountain for all your block needs. Just watch out as you descend – there could be a hollow cave below you!

9 FARMING

Next, create some farmland by placing dirt blocks around a water source and hoeing it. Plant your wheat seeds and wait for your crops to grow. Keep extending your farm until you have enough wheat to always keep your hunger bar full.

11 PAVEMENTS

Create a safe space for your home – that means getting rid of that slippery ice! Using blocks from your mining expedition, start replacing the ground blocks with sturdy stone slabs until you've cleared an area large enough for your home.

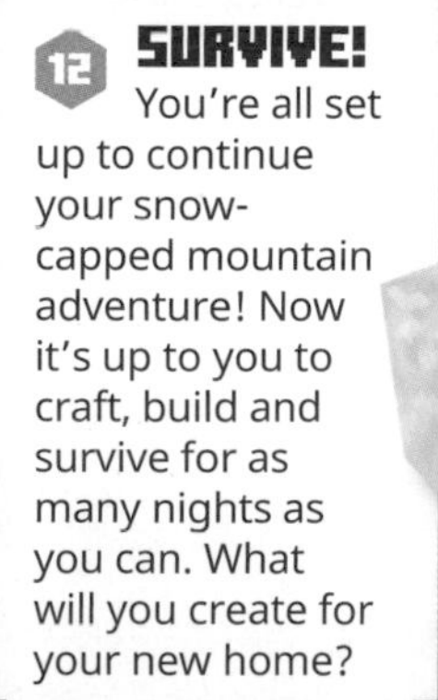

12 SURVIVE!

You're all set up to continue your snow-capped mountain adventure! Now it's up to you to craft, build and survive for as many nights as you can. What will you create for your new home?

BECOME A MINECRAFT CREATOR

Ever dreamed of becoming a Minecraft content creator? Lucky for us, Mojang Studios have released a new learning portal to help new and experienced creators make content for Minecraft. Let's take a closer look at some of the things you can do on this shiny new website.

WHAT IS A MINECRAFT CREATOR?

A creator is anyone who makes content for Minecraft, whether it's skin textures, worlds, videos, memes – the list goes on and on. If you made it yourself, you're a creator!

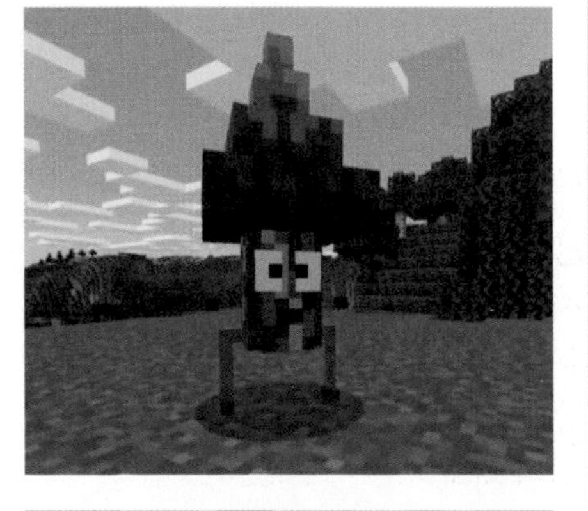

LEARNING PORTAL

Visit www.minecraft.net/en-us/creator to see how Minecraft content creation works and find the resources you need to learn how to become a creator. There are tons of guides to help get you started and a new documentation site that allows you to delve deep into all the components and entities in Minecraft.

GETTING STARTED: MINECRAFT ENTITY WIZARD

Not sure where to start? Why not design your own mob? On a PC or Mac, you can use the same software that Mojang used to create the axolotl mob.

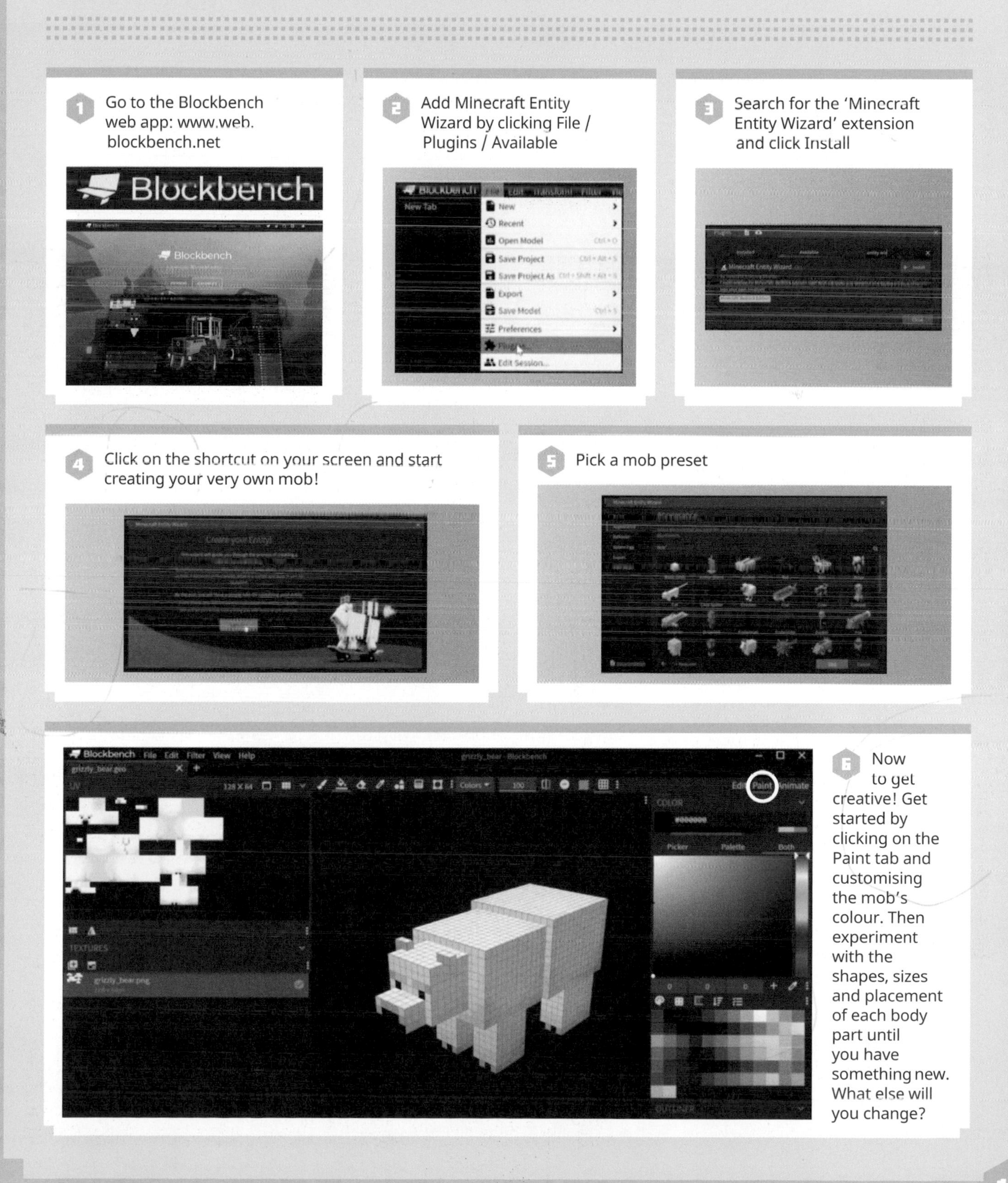

1 Go to the Blockbench web app: www.web.blockbench.net

2 Add Minecraft Entity Wizard by clicking File / Plugins / Available

3 Search for the 'Minecraft Entity Wizard' extension and click Install

4 Click on the shortcut on your screen and start creating your very own mob!

5 Pick a mob preset

6 Now to get creative! Get started by clicking on the Paint tab and customising the mob's colour. Then experiment with the shapes, sizes and placement of each body part until you have something new. What else will you change?

SPOT THE DIFFERENCE
THE WARDEN

Rumours have reached us of a fierce mob that lurks in the deep dark: the warden. Although few have ever set eyes on this mob and survived, it is said that though it cannot see, it is capable of detecting vibrations. Explorers have captured two images of this mysterious mob in the wild. Can you spot the ten differences between them?

1 ⬡ 2 ⬡ 3 ⬡ 4 ⬡ 5 ⬡ 6 ⬡ 7 ⬡ 8 ⬡ 9 ⬡ 10 ⬡

Check your answers on page 68

UNDERWATER BUILD CHALLENGE

There's a whole world hidden beneath the surface of the ocean. Dolphins, tropical fish, shipwrecks, ruins. Even monuments overrun by guardians! It's a dangerous place, but it's worth exploring. Prepare yourself for some deep-sea adventures with this underwater base. Find out how to build yourself a fish farm on page 23.

1 GLASS WINDOWS

Build your underwater base using glass windows so you can see the biome around you. Drowned cannot break glass, so you're completely safe from those ocean-dwelling mobs.

4 SEA LANTERNS

Add sea lanterns to your build. They will illuminate the base and help it stand out in the depths, making it easy to spot when you return from exploring. You can also create perimeter lights to help guide you from afar.

2 FOOD FARM

Finding food underwater can be time-consuming. Creating a fish farm will make this much easier. Use magma, hoppers and chests to catch and cook all the fish you could need!

3 THEY'RE S'CUTE!

Breed nearby turtles using seagrass to collect scutes. Scutes can be used to create turtle helmets that allow you to breathe underwater, a useful buff to have while working toward your conduit.

5 CONDUIT POWER

Building a conduit will help immensely with your underwater survival. Conduits restore oxygen, provide underwater night vision and increase mining speed to nearby players. They will also damage nearby hostile mobs to help you stay safe. You'll need to find a heart of the sea in buried treasure, and create the conduit structure with prismarine blocks to unlock its power.

8 CORAL REEF

Venture below the surface of the ocean and find a coral reef. They can be found in warm ocean biomes. Coral reefs are full of sea pickles that will light up the area around you.

7 SPONGES

If you see a monument nearby, search inside for sponges. They can be used to quickly drain water. Once they're wet, simply place them in a furnace to dry them out again.

6 AIRLOCK

Use an airlock to get in and out of the base without water flooding in. This can be done by creating a water gate – a gate made using blocks that stop water from flowing in. This one is made using two doors.

UNDERWATER BUILD CHALLENGE

PART 2

BUILDING WITH SPARKS

BUBBLE COLUMNS

Bubble columns from underwater magma blocks will pull down anything that passes above them – such as fish! The fish will then get cooked on the hot magma and collected into the chest below by the minecart with a hopper.

TOP TIP

If you want a bubble column that pushes upwards, replace the magma blocks for soul sand. This will push anything above it towards the surface.

UNDERWATER FOOD FARM

0.5 HRS 1 2 3 4 MODERATE

Building an underwater food farm is the best way to ensure survival below the ocean. This farm will not only catch you fish, but also cook them for you to quickly restore your hunger bar. Place deep in the ocean to ensure you catch plenty of fish above it. You'll find cod in normal and cold oceans, and salmon in cold and frozen oceans, and rivers.

BUILD TIP

Bubble columns need a water source above each magma block to work. If the bubbles are not appearing, use a bucket and place a water source atop each of the magma blocks. If the bubbles don't go to the surface, it means there's a water source missing.

5 blocks

5 blocks

magma blocks

minecart with hopper

rail

lever

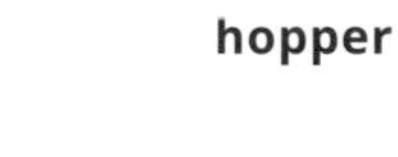

powered rail

hopper

chest

3 blocks

3 blocks

MEET MOJANG STUDIOS

When it comes to creating new blocks, biomes and mobs for Minecraft, the team at Mojang Studios is a well-oiled machine. From game designers and gameplay developers to community managers and creative writers, each member of the team plays a vital role in making incredible new Minecraft features. We asked them, of the new features, what do they love most?

AXOLOTL

mac, Engineering Manager for Minecraft Java Edition

It's an animal that is not (well ... WAS not) in the collective imagination like the other animals we added before, so it expands the knowledge of our players. It is also an endangered species and an animal of significance for the culture it is a native of, and I find it important for Minecraft to give visibility to both. It is also extremely cute ...

MUSIC

Adrian Östergård, Producer

Music and sound is one of my absolute favourite things in any game, and the huge music addition we did in Caves & Cliffs: Part II was great. This is also the first time in eight years we added new music to the main menu. It was just mind-blowing to hear something else in there.

TRIDENT

Steve Enos, Game Designer

The trident is the perfect tool for an undersea adventurer. With the Riptide and Loyalty enchantments, the player can choose between a magical force that boosts you through the water and rain, or a ranged weapon with infinite ammo, or just carry both. Also, when it's stormy outside, you can call down lightning on every mob you hit with the Channeling enchantment. You'll have charged creepers for days!

SPYGLASS

Felix Jones, Java Game Developer

I can use it to see things very far away, and it is a great accessory for pretending to be a pirate with my friends.

CONCRETE BLOCKS

Zach Bowman, Gameplay Systems Engineer

I use concrete in almost all of my survival buildings. It's easy to make and it's so nice being able to make a house that's red, blue or purple without making it all out of wool. Those wool houses don't mix well with creepers!

WANDERING TRADER

Per Landin, Creative Writer & Editor, Minecraft.net

The wandering trader is a spontaneous fellow that shows up when you least expect them, always together with a trusty llama or two. I just love the idea of a visitor from lands far, far away coming to pay the player a visit to trade goods. It makes the world feel vibrant and alive.

DRIPSTONE-FILLED CAULDRONS

Tyler Laing, Senior Software Development Lead

I proposed this fun idea to our game designers, and they improved it by introducing renewable lava source blocks!

COPPER

Jifeng Zhang, Technical Director

I am a big fan of history. With copper, I can add a historical aspect to my buildings.

MEET MOJANG STUDIOS

PART 2

BEES

Cojo, Gameplay Developer

Bees are so much fun to have around. They add so much ambience and teach players of the many benefits bees provide to us in real life.

DROWNED

Matt Gartzke, Community Manager

Making parts of the drowned glow helped make them much scarier mobs. It's frightening to look down into the depths of the ocean and see the glowing eyes of the undead!

WATERLOGGING & UNDERWATER BUILDING

Anthony 'Sunken City' Cloudy, Gameplay Developer

Minecraft was built with the idea of one block per space, but when we wanted to make it possible to build underwater, we struggled with this rule! Sometimes when working on a game, you have to rework your previous ideas into something new to keep moving forwards. By challenging what we had thought of as 'just the way things were', our team was able to make it possible to build underwater cities, sculptures or anything you could imagine! It was a good life lesson: don't be afraid to experiment and rework what you've done in order to make your dreams come true!

TERRAIN GENERATION

Michal Nowak, QA Test Associate

The new generation added in the Caves & Cliffs positively changes how the game feels. The mountains are a wonder to look at and the vast underwater cave systems are awesome to explore. Oh, and the axolotls ... CUTE! As a tester, it is an amazing feeling to be part of this huge update.

REALMS

Bill Klees, Senior Software Engineer

Realms has made it so easy to play Minecraft with your friends. Whether you play on PC, console or mobile, you can create a new world and be playing and building together in no time! Already have an existing world? You can upload it to Realms and invite all your friends to check it out.

BEES!

John Littlewood, Software Developer, Games Foundation

I just love bees! I think they're a perfect fit in Minecraft – super cute, hard-working and give you something really sweet! But there's also a little bit of danger there too ... exactly like Minecraft as a whole – always an adventure!

GAMETYPES

Joining a Minecraft server is a great way to experience the game with friends. There are tons of ways to play, with more gametypes and minigames being offered on servers all the time. Let's take a look at some of the most popular gametypes being played.

SURVIVAL

The original gametype – Survival mode! Play with friends, explore the Overworld, gather resources and build bases. Discover the fundamentals of playing the game, alongside a community of similar-minded players.

CAPTURE THE FLAG

This gametype splits players into two teams. Each team has a flag, and players must find, capture and bring the enemy team's flag back to their own base to win the game. It will be a fiercely fought PVP battle as each team fights to bring the flags one step closer to their base.

PARKOUR

Hop, skip and jump your way across challenging obstacles to reach the end. You'll have to time your jumps perfectly, aim arrows accurately and glide smoothly using elytra to reach the end – will you make it or will you be walking back to the starting line?

FACTIONS

Another gametype where players are split into two teams. In this game, each team must build bases and strive to survive while keeping an eye out for enemy players launching raids. Better keep your swords ready and those diamonds locked up securely!

SKYWARS

Skywars pits four teams against each other in this limited resource, sky-high block challenge. Each team starts on its own sky island, and it's up to the players to reinforce defences or build bridges to attack other islands. The last team standing wins the war.

PRISON

Wake up in prison and and work your way up the ranks of prison society! In this gametype, you'll have to mine for resources to climb the social ladder. Rise high enough and you'll walk free!

TIPS & TRICKS

EXPERT GUIDE WITH MONTY

Did you know that there are over 600 unique blocks, items and mobs in Minecraft? That's a lot! Every year, Minecraft is updated with more and more for players to enjoy. With so many additions over time, there are countless details that you can make great use of. Let's take a look at some of them here!

EXPLOSIVE FEET

Tired of being blown up by creepers? This trick might just be the one for you! When creepers explode, the damage is done to your feet. By placing a block on the ground between you and the exploding creeper, you can greatly reduce the damage received.

MOB-PROOF GATES

Keeping mobs locked in pens is a frustrating task. They keep escaping when you open the gate, and when you've finally rounded them up, somehow another one gets out. It's impossible! Or is it? You can create mob-proof gates using a gate and fences. Simply place a gate with two fences behind it like this.

NO DARKNESS = NO MOBS!

A simple but also important tip: lighting prevents mobs from spawning! Mobs only spawn on blocks that are in total darkness, so place torches to keep yourself safe from hostile mobs.

THIRD PERSON

If you're travelling on a boat and want to see underwater, or wearing a pumpkin head in the End, change your perspective to the third person view by pressing F5 or selecting it in your settings, which will allow you to look around your character.

GRAVEL & SAND

Did you know that the most effective way to gather gravel and sand is NOT with a shovel? Don't worry, you won't be using your fists either. Gravel and sand are gravity blocks that fall – but they cannot fall into a space already occupied. If you place a torch under a column of gravel or sand and break the block above it, the column will fall and break on the torch.

CROSSBOW AIM

Everyone loves a good trick shot! You can impress your friends with some impeccable aim using this trick: put your spyglass in your offhand and load your crossbow, then use the spyglass to aim. You'll be hitting the bullseye from a distance in no time.

DIVE DEEPER

With more than ten years of history, Minecraft is packed with mysteries. While much knowledge has been passed down through the years from player to player, many secrets have become lost to time. How well do you know your Minecraft trivia? Have you heard of all these facts?

MEOW!
MEOW!

TRIVIA #2

MEOW MEOW

Ghast noises can be terrifying in the Nether – but did you know they were voiced by a sleeping cat? Bet they don't seem so terrifying anymore!

TRIVIA #1

FRIEND OR FOE?

If you're caught in a tough spot and need a way out, you can name a vindicator Johnny and it'll turn into a raging mob that attacks all nearby mobs with an axe. Including you! Make sure to plan your escape first.

EASTER EGG

The Minecraft creators love to include Easter eggs, which are secret details hidden in the game as a surprise for players who stumble across them. They can be images, text messages or even rampaging vindicators! Keep an eye out!

GIANT ZOMBIE

If you thought zombies were scary, just wait until you see a giant zombie in Java Edition! You won't find them naturally in the game, but you can spawn one using this command: /summon minecraft:giant. Luckily, this big green monster is harmless.

TRIVIA #3

ENDERMEN EYES

As many unfortunate Minecrafters know, Endermen hate when you look into their piercing purple eyes. Did you know they were originally green? Perhaps that's why the eye of Ender is green instead of purple.

BOOSTED FOX

Did you know that foxes can carry items in their mouths and that a fox's main hand is also its mouth? You can combine these to create a boosted fox. Simply give a fox a diamond sword and it will be granted bonus damage, boosting its standard attack.

MARKETPLACE

EXPERT GUIDE WITH BEAR

Looking for a new way to enjoy Minecraft? The marketplace has you covered! There are tons of packs you can download that will completely change the way you play. From new themes and adventures to custom-made Survival worlds, there's a pack to suit everyone's needs on the Marketplace.

ADVENTURE MAPS

Discover a whole new adventure, solo or with friends, in these incredible maps created to immerse you in a story!

SWEET DEFENSE

BY HUMBLEBRIGHT STUDIO

This one is for anyone with a sweet tooth – be warned, though, it can trigger sugar cravings! Not all is as it seems at the Honey Festival. You and your friends must defend the Hive in this surprisingly action-packed minigame. How cute!

DIVERSITY

BY ZOMBOCRON

Do you love conquering enemies, putting your trivia knowledge to the test, racing mates parkour-style and solving puzzles? We sure do! This game has it all! Put your skills to the ultimate test with this epic adventure map.

GOOD TROUBLE

BY MINECRAFT

Are you a warrior for justice? Embark on a journey through history alongside famous leaders and learn how there's such a thing as 'good trouble'. Come along and explore how you, too, can change the world for the better!

THE THEME PARK

BY OREVILLE STUDIOS

Can't get to a theme park in real life? No problem! You can help restore this one to its former glory, by exploring the Fantasy Kingdom, Pirate Cove and more, completing challenges and mini-games to earn tickets. It's so much fun!

TEXTURE PACKS

Embrace a new creative challenge with an awesome new texture pack, which will change the look of certain blocks, mobs and skins!

ALLEGRO

BY PIXEL SQUARED

This pack gives your game a fresh new look with a cheerful pixel art style! Watch the cute animals, mobs and villagers roam as you munch on delicious foods. There are even five new skins to dress up your character with, which we adore!

ADVENTURE

BY BLOCKCEPTION

We love how this pack brings a more natural and earthy feeling to the world, with its unique textures and outfits. It's perfect for creating a more historical or real-world feel in the game.

THE MILKY WAY

BY GIGGLE BLOCK STUDIOS

This pack is out of this world! These bright colours and spacesuit skins are awesome for creating a unique futuristic world that's like nothing you've ever seen before. It's seriously cool!

STITCHED TOGETHER

BY TEAM VISIONARY

Even the mobs have been sewn up into new outfits in this pack! We love the way it makes everything look like it's made from woven cloth. It's super cosy and full of bright colours that will transform your world!

BIOHAZARD

BY ODD BLOCK

This pack will turn your world into an apocalyptic wasteland filled with creepy mobs. Amazing, right? We like how it puts your survival skills to the test and gives the game a new look that feels really edgy.

KAWAII ANIME

BY GIGGLE BLOCK STUDIOS

You can't get much cuter than this texture pack. We couldn't get over how adorable the mobs are with their huge anime-style eyes. We're sure you'll be smitten too!

MARKETPLACE

SURVIVAL SPAWNS

Put your survival skills to the ultimate test and immerse yourself in a whole new world with these carefully crafted survival spawn packs.

MORE ORES

BY BBB STUDIOS

If you enjoy mining, we think you'll adore this. This survival pack is full to the brim of awesome new ores to collect, as well as vehicles, tools and parkour to try out. What are you waiting for? Get digging!

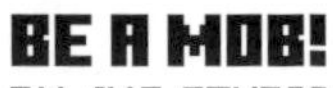

BE A MOB!

BY 4KS STUDIOS

Do you love mobs? Us too! In this pack, you can be whichever one you want. We enjoy exploring the Overworld in mob form – flying as a bee, swimming as a dolphin and climbing as a spider. Which will you try first?

JUNGLE WARRIORS

BY DIVEBLOCKS

We love battling through these amazing jungle dungeons in this intense survival game. If the thrill of successfully fending off hordes of mobs wasn't enjoyable enough, you also get magic wands!

SPY MOBS SCHOOL

BY OWLS CUBED

Who doesn't dream of being a spy at one point? Spies are cool! In this pack, you get to go to spy school and battle it out against your mates to become the best spy in class. Don't worry – these lessons are far from boring!

HACKER SCHOOL ROLEPLAY

BY BLOCKLAB STUDIOS

This one's for the computer lovers out there. Sure, going to school might seem lame, but trust us, this pack is anything but! You get to learn about computer science while role-playing as a nifty hacker in the game.

MASH-UPS

Mash-up packs let you modify your Minecraft world with new skins, textures and maps. Enjoy a fresh new look with one of these awesome themes!

MUTANT MASH-UP

BY EVERBLOOM GAMES

This mash-up is a wild ride through a huge apocalyptic city – driving crazy cars, completing quests and figuring out what happened there. We love how fun and immersive this map is.

LUCKY PLANTS

BY TEPLIGHT STUDIOS

If you thought the Lucky Block mod was awesome, think again. This pack allows you to grow lucky plants! Plant your seeds and see what incredible plants you get. It's surprisingly addictive.

TOYS MASH-UP

BY TEAM VISIONARY

We've all had that fantasy where our toys come to life – well, in this mash-up, they actually are! We enjoy how the toys each have their own lives and personalities – it's seriously cute.

INTERSELLAR CITY BUILDER MASH-UP

BY ATHERIS GAMES

Space, robots, vehicles, new furniture: what more could you want? This pack has you building a futuristic colony on a far-away planet. It's a building map like no other – we love how creative you can get with it!

CUTE MASH-UP

BY VOXELBLOCKS

As the name suggests, this one is seriously cute! Make your world miniature, surround yourself with adorable mobs and set off to explore pirate ships and skull islands. Who could resist that? Not us!

MINECRAFT JOKES

Think you can match all of these Minecraft jokes with their correct answers? When you're done, see if you can make your friends laugh.

Check your answers on page 68

COMMAND BLOCK 101

Change the weather, give yourself a full set of netherite armour, flood your inventory with emeralds and many more possibilities, all at the press of a button. Command blocks are super powerful and special blocks that can execute commands as you play, making them a great tool to deploy. Read our guide so you can learn how to make them part of your Minecraft life.

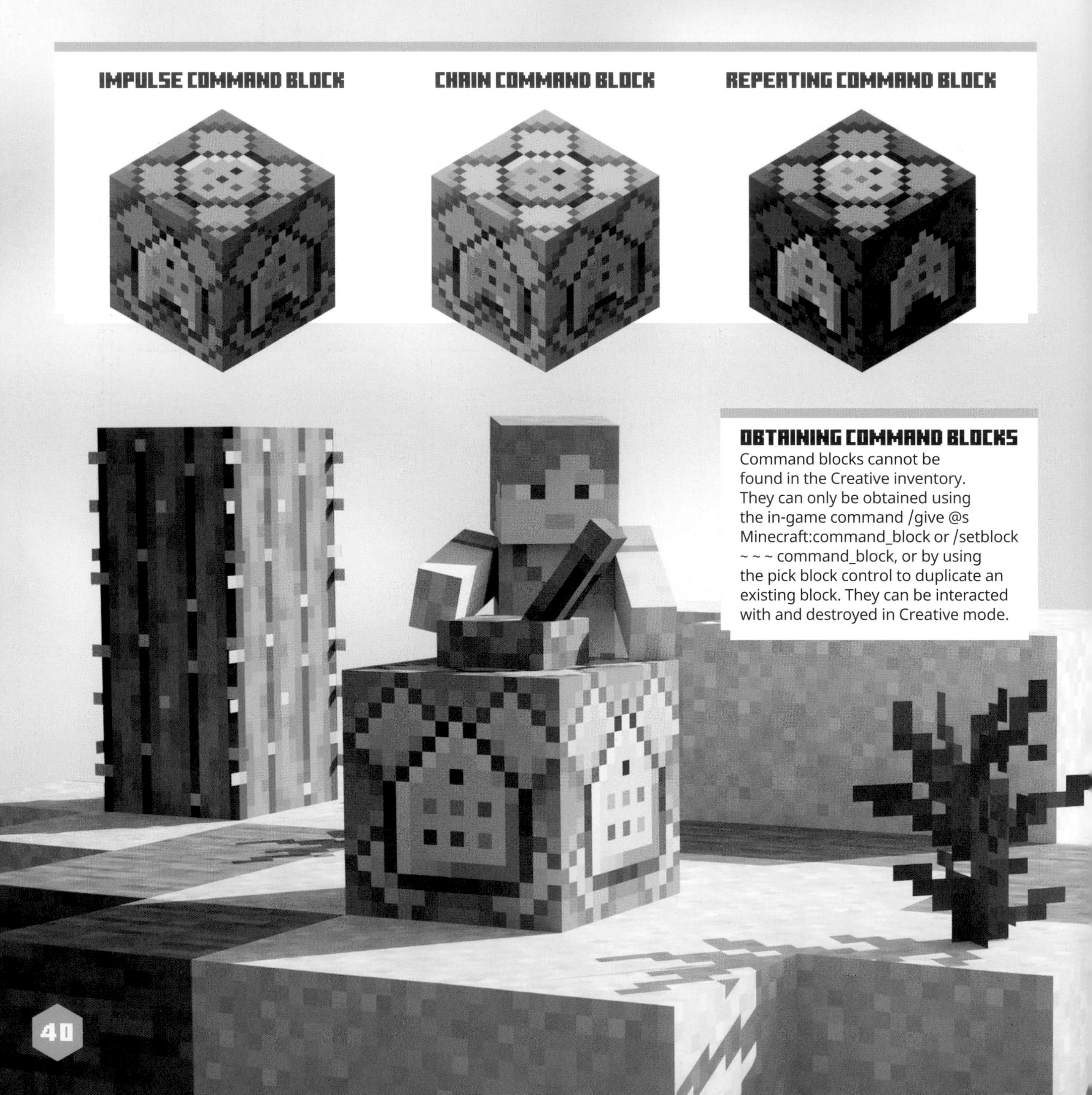

OBTAINING COMMAND BLOCKS

Command blocks cannot be found in the Creative inventory. They can only be obtained using the in-game command /give @s Minecraft:command_block or /setblock ~ ~ ~ command_block, or by using the pick block control to duplicate an existing block. They can be interacted with and destroyed in Creative mode.

COMMAND BLOCK GUI

This is the command block user interface in Bedrock Edition. How you set your options will determine how the command block functions. Each of these are described below:

The block type determines what kind of command block it is:

IMPULSE
An impulse command block will execute a command once it's powered by a redstone signal.

REPEATING
A repeating command block will continue to execute the command repeatedly for as long as it has a redstone signal.

CHAIN
Chain command blocks carry a pulse, allowing you to activate multiple command blocks together. Chain command blocks must be set to Always Active.

The condition toggle determines the blocks' behaviour:

CONDITIONAL
Conditional commands will only execute if the command before it has already been implemented.

UNCONDITIONAL
Unconditional commands will always execute regardless of whether the command before it has been performed.

DELAY IN TICKS
Choose how long to wait from activating the command block to executing the command or, in the case of the repeating command block, how long it takes to do it again.

YOUR COMMAND
Enter your command here to determine the purpose of your block and what it does.

COMMAND TARGETS
Just as with in-game commands, you will need to specify which player(s) the command will effect.

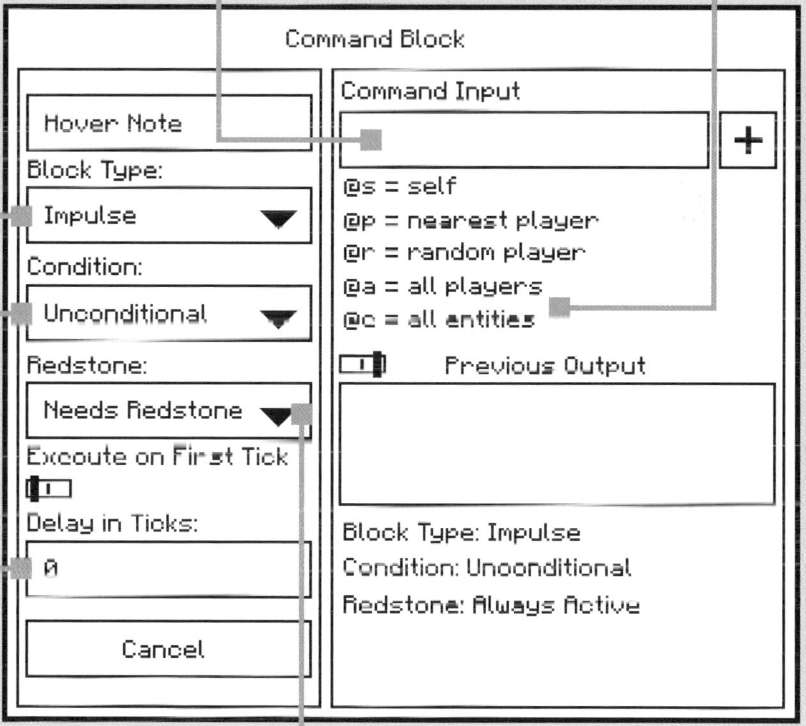

The redstone toggle determines how the block is activated:

ALWAYS ACTIVE
Always Active will continue to execute a command on loop. It is always active, even without redstone.

NEEDS REDSTONE
Needs Redstone means that the block will only activate when triggered by a redstone signal.

COMMAND BLOCK 101
BASIC CONTRAPTIONS

If you found all that information hard to process, you're not the only one! Understanding command blocks can be challenging. The best way to get familiar with them is to get some practice. Try the examples below to get started. When you get them to work, try playing around with the settings to see how you can change them.

SETTING THE TIME

Let's start with simple impulse command blocks that control day and night in your Minecraft world using the Time command.

1 In the console text box, type in '/give @s minecraft:command_block'.

```
/give @s minecraft:command_block
```

2 Place two command blocks and label them 'DAY' and 'NIGHT'.

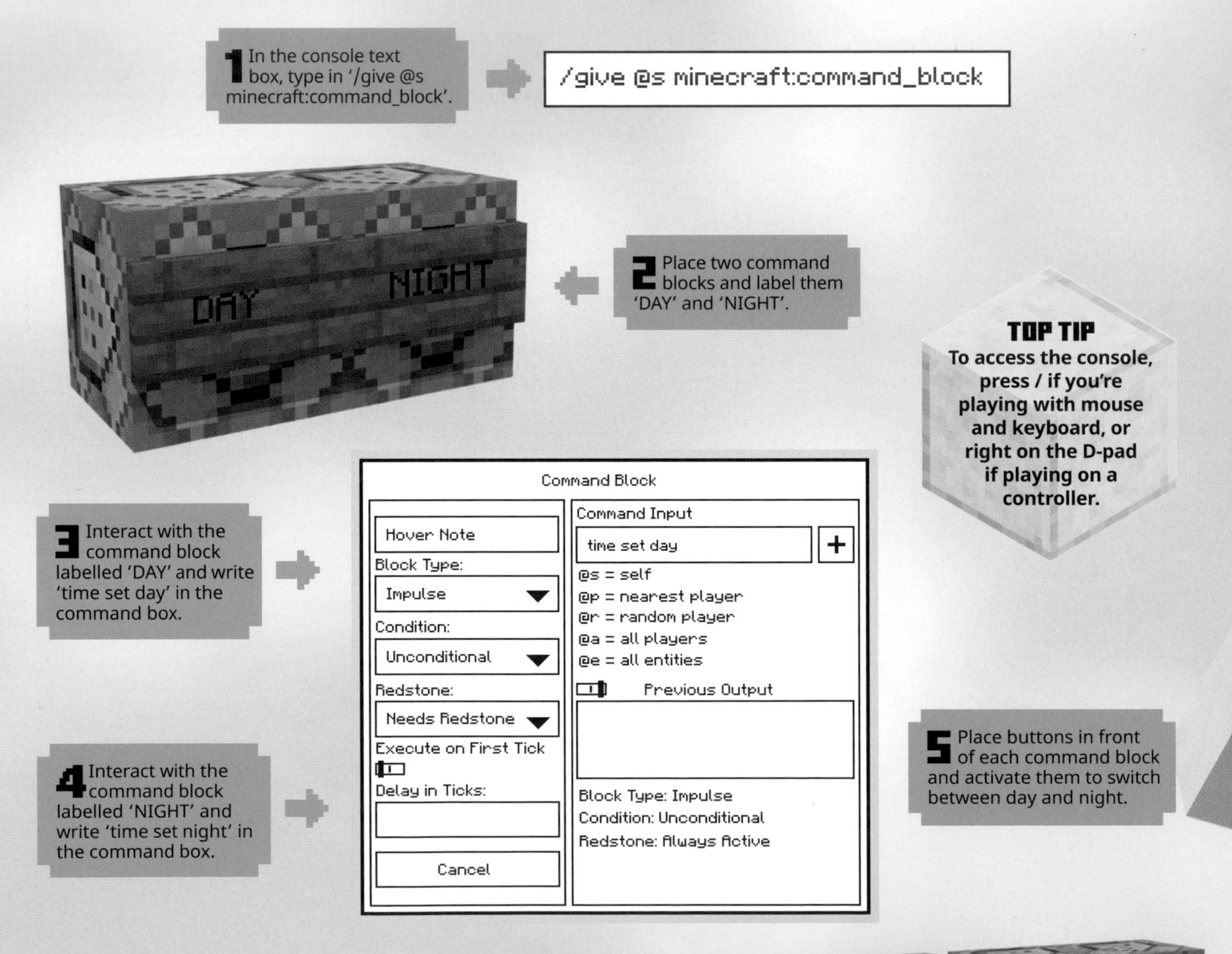

3 Interact with the command block labelled 'DAY' and write 'time set day' in the command box.

4 Interact with the command block labelled 'NIGHT' and write 'time set night' in the command box.

5 Place buttons in front of each command block and activate them to switch between day and night.

TOP TIP

To access the console, press / if you're playing with mouse and keyboard, or right on the D-pad if playing on a controller.

CHANGE DIFFICULTY

Now that you know how to create a simple impulse command, can you work out how to change the difficulty? Try creating impulse commands to change between Peaceful, Easy, Normal and Hard modes. Hint: use the Difficulty command.

GIVE AN ITEM

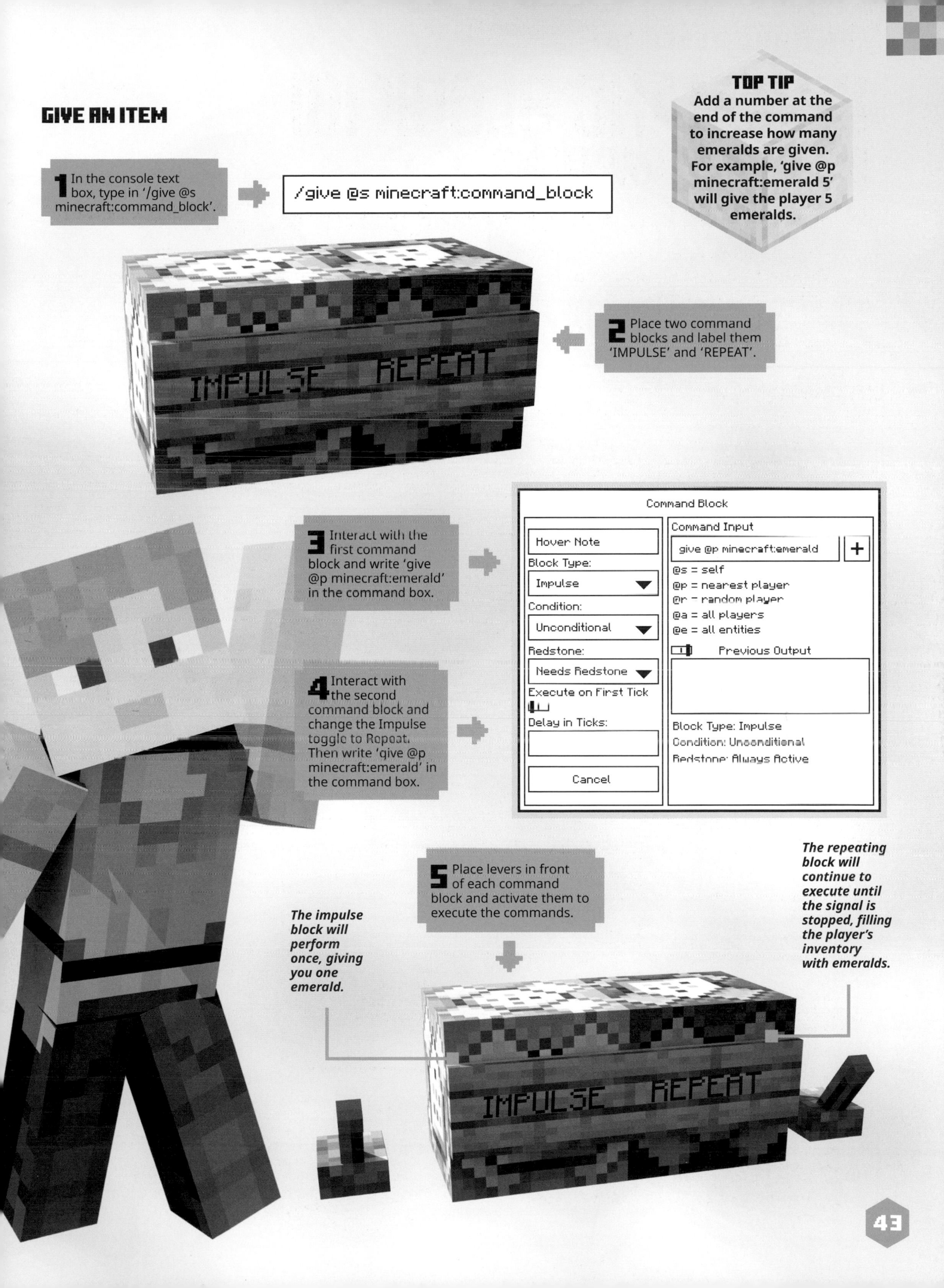

TOP TIP

Add a number at the end of the command to increase how many emeralds are given. For example, 'give @p minecraft:emerald 5' will give the player 5 emeralds.

1 In the console text box, type in '/give @s minecraft:command_block'.

2 Place two command blocks and label them 'IMPULSE' and 'REPEAT'.

3 Interact with the first command block and write 'give @p minecraft:emerald' in the command box.

4 Interact with the second command block and change the Impulse toggle to Repeat. Then write 'give @p minecraft:emerald' in the command box.

5 Place levers in front of each command block and activate them to execute the commands.

The impulse block will perform once, giving you one emerald.

The repeating block will continue to execute until the signal is stopped, filling the player's inventory with emeralds.

SUMMON A MOB

1 In the console text box, type in '/give @s minecraft:command_block'.

2 Place a command block and label it 'SUMMON'.

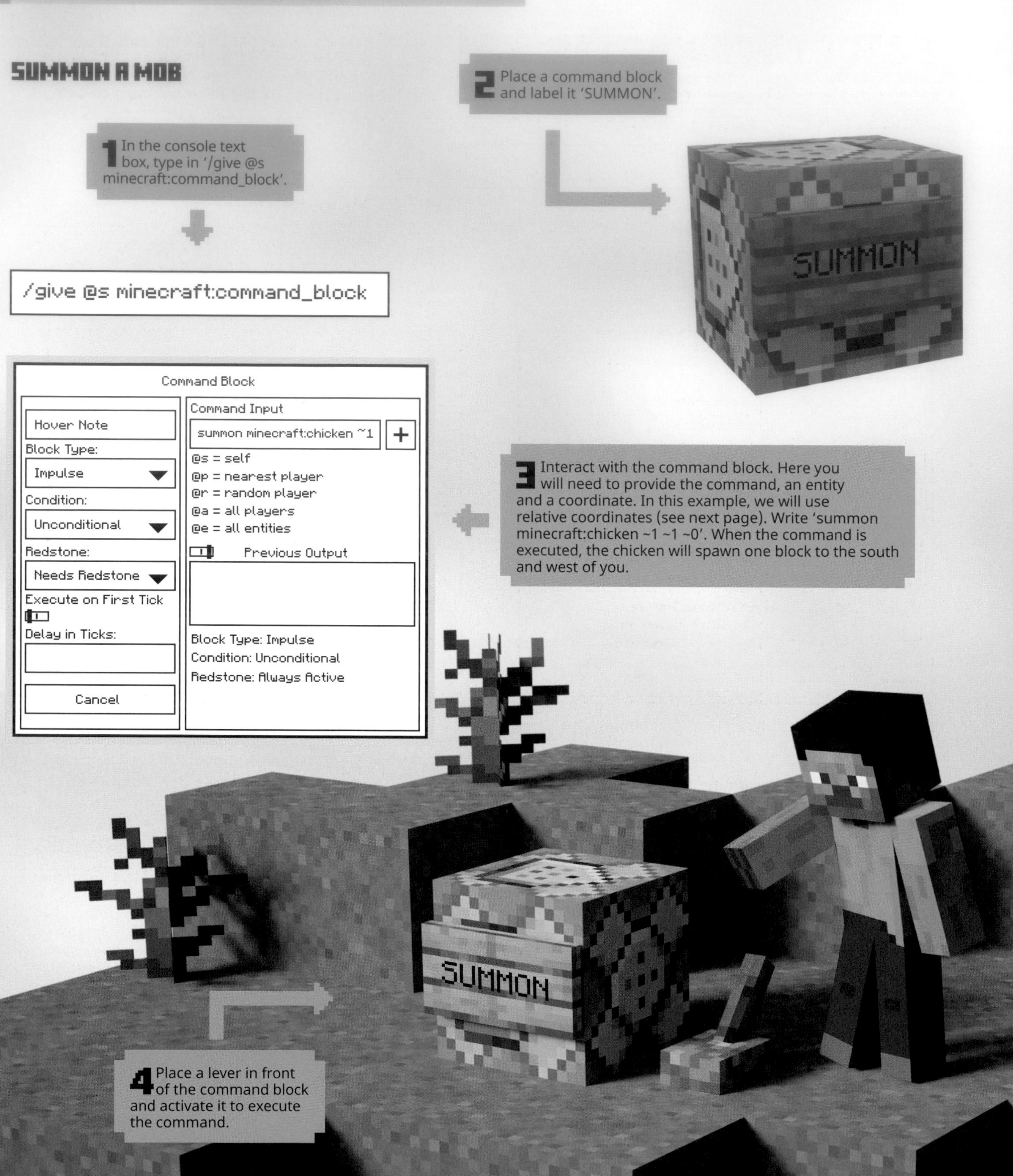

3 Interact with the command block. Here you will need to provide the command, an entity and a coordinate. In this example, we will use relative coordinates (see next page). Write 'summon minecraft:chicken ~1 ~1 ~0'. When the command is executed, the chicken will spawn one block to the south and west of you.

4 Place a lever in front of the command block and activate it to execute the command.

EXPERIMENT!

Now it's time for you to experiment! See if you can use the Fill command. With the Fill command, you will need to provide two sets of coordinates. Try using this command and see what you can create: 'fill ~1 ~1 ~1 ~5 ~1 ~1 minecraft:stone'. Notice how the second set of coordinates is 5? Change the numbers to see how it affects the command.

EXACT COORDINATES & RELATIVE COORDINATES

Coordinates represent the location of every block in your world in an XYZ format. In Bedrock Edition, you can see these by selecting the Show Coordinates option in the settings. When inputting a command that requires coordinates, you have two options: exact coordinates or relative coordinates.

EXACT COORDINATES

Exact coordinates correspond to a specific block location in your world. For example, to summon a chicken at the coordinates XYZ: 300 / 40 / 250, you would use the exact coordinates in your command: 'summon minecraft:chicken 300 40 250'.

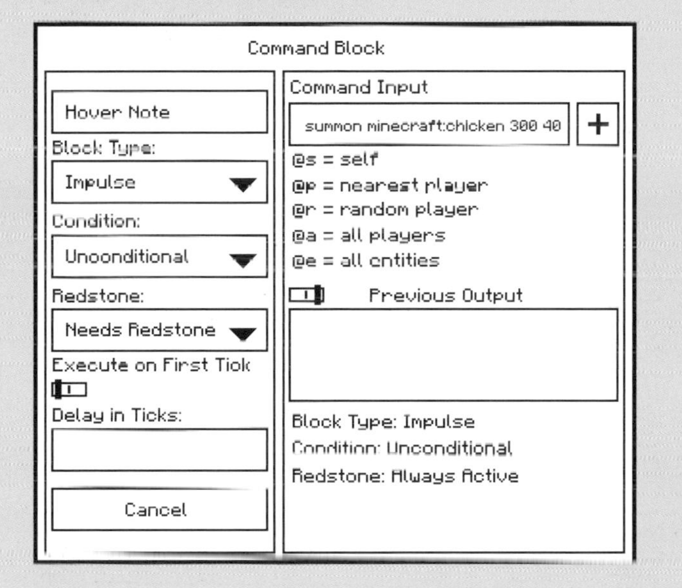

RELATIVE COORDINATES

Relative coordinates correspond to a specific block location relation to the command block. Simply input how far from the command block the coordinate is. For example, to summon a chicken 5 blocks from the command block, you would use the relative coordinates 'summon minecraft:chicken ~ ~ ~5'

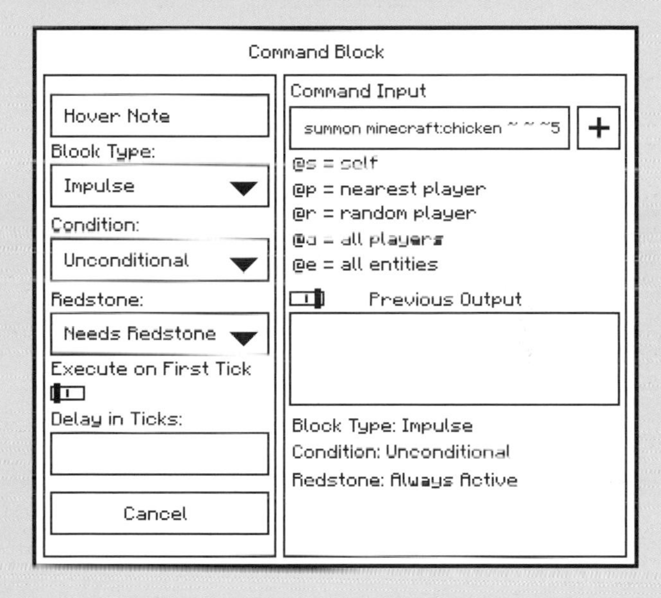

FIND MORE RESOURCES ONLINE

This guide will introduce you to command blocks, but it's only the start of your journey. There is a lot more you can do with these incredibly useful blocks. To learn more, check out the many online tutorials.

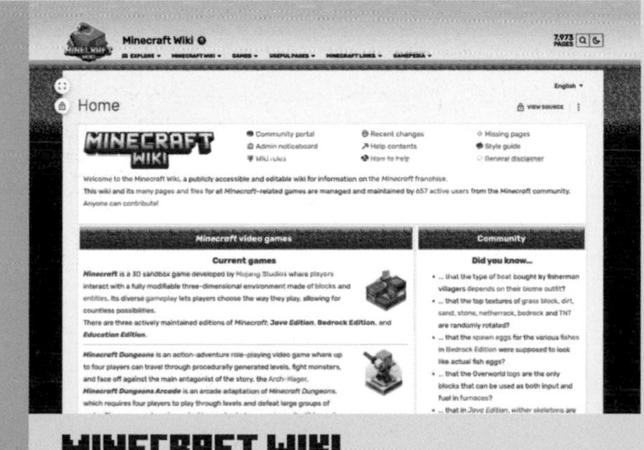

MINECRAFT WIKI

The Minecraft Wiki contains a trove of information for players, including many command block tutorials. Head to https://minecraft.fandom.com/ to find out more.

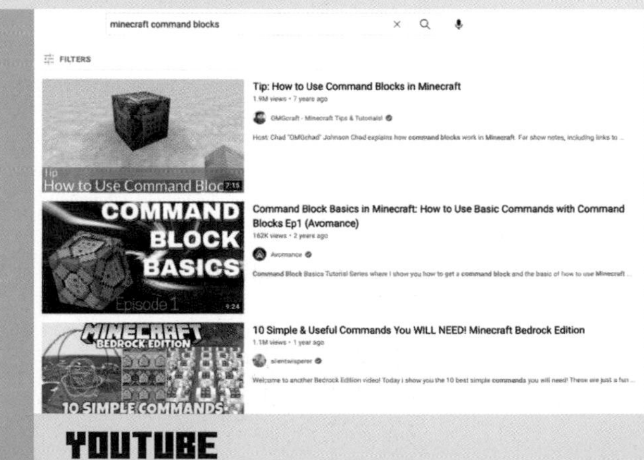

YOUTUBE

Discover countless detailed guides and tutorials on command blocks by the Minecraft community on YouTube. If you get stuck, you'll likely find a helpful video explaining what you need to do on this platform.

BLOCK BY BLOCK: MIND THE STEP

Minecraft's potential is endless, and some organisations are using it to achieve incredible goals. Block by Block is a foundation run by Mojang, Microsoft and UN-Habitat that helps communities have a say in how their neighbourhoods are built. They use Minecraft to design spaces that solve problems around them, and then present their ideas to the city planners and architects, so they can be built for real!

BREAKING DOWN INVISIBLE BARRIERS

Around the world, from Kosovo to Mozambique, the foundation aims to break down barriers by using Minecraft as a place where everyone can think about their buildings and environment, and exchange their ideas visually, in the most inclusive way possible.

Minecraft helps local people, including children, city officials, architects and planners find a common language, so everyone understands each other. It's a simple, fun platform that everyone can get involved in.

So, as well as helping them improve the world around them, Minecraft also shows how everyone, even young kids, can have a future as architects, urban planners and politicians. It also introduces community members to using computers to explain their ideas and find answers to their problems!

BLOCK BY BLOCK™

BUILDING COMMON GROUND

To find out more about Block by Block and their work, head to www.blockbyblock.org, where you can learn more about their past and ongoing projects, and how you too can get involved.

CASE STUDY: SAO PAULO

Recently, Block by Block worked with Mind the Step to help improve safety and mobility in low-income neighbourhoods in Sao Paolo, Brazil. By revitalising the city's public staircases, they became safer and more enjoyable places to be in.

The initiative, created by Cidade Ativa and known as Mind the Step, identified the large number of public staircases as an opportunity to get the locals exercising more regularly. The city didn't have space for many parks, so these staircases were also seen as places that could be used for outdoor communal areas and playgrounds.

In 2018, a staircase in a poor area called Jardim Nakamura was chosen to be redesigned. Even though the staircase is very useful because it leads to shops and a busy bus stop, people living there weren't using it because it was in such bad repair.

Locals, particularly children, were invited to get involved in redesigning the staircase on Minecraft, and together they decided to add mural paintings, a slide, benches and a community library and board. Today the space is a safer space and the number of users has drastically increased, especially in children.

ANIMAL EXPERT

Mobs come in all shapes and sizes, but how well do you know your animal mobs? Test your knowledge to see if you know everything there is to know about Minecraft's many loveable creatures.

1 What do you get when you breed a blue sheep and a red sheep?

ANSWER ....

2 What valuable item do baby turtles shed when they grow up?

ANSWER ....

3 How do you calm a bee?

ANSWER ....

4 What food can you use to breed goats?

ANSWER ....

5 What conditions do axolotls need to spawn?

ANSWER ....

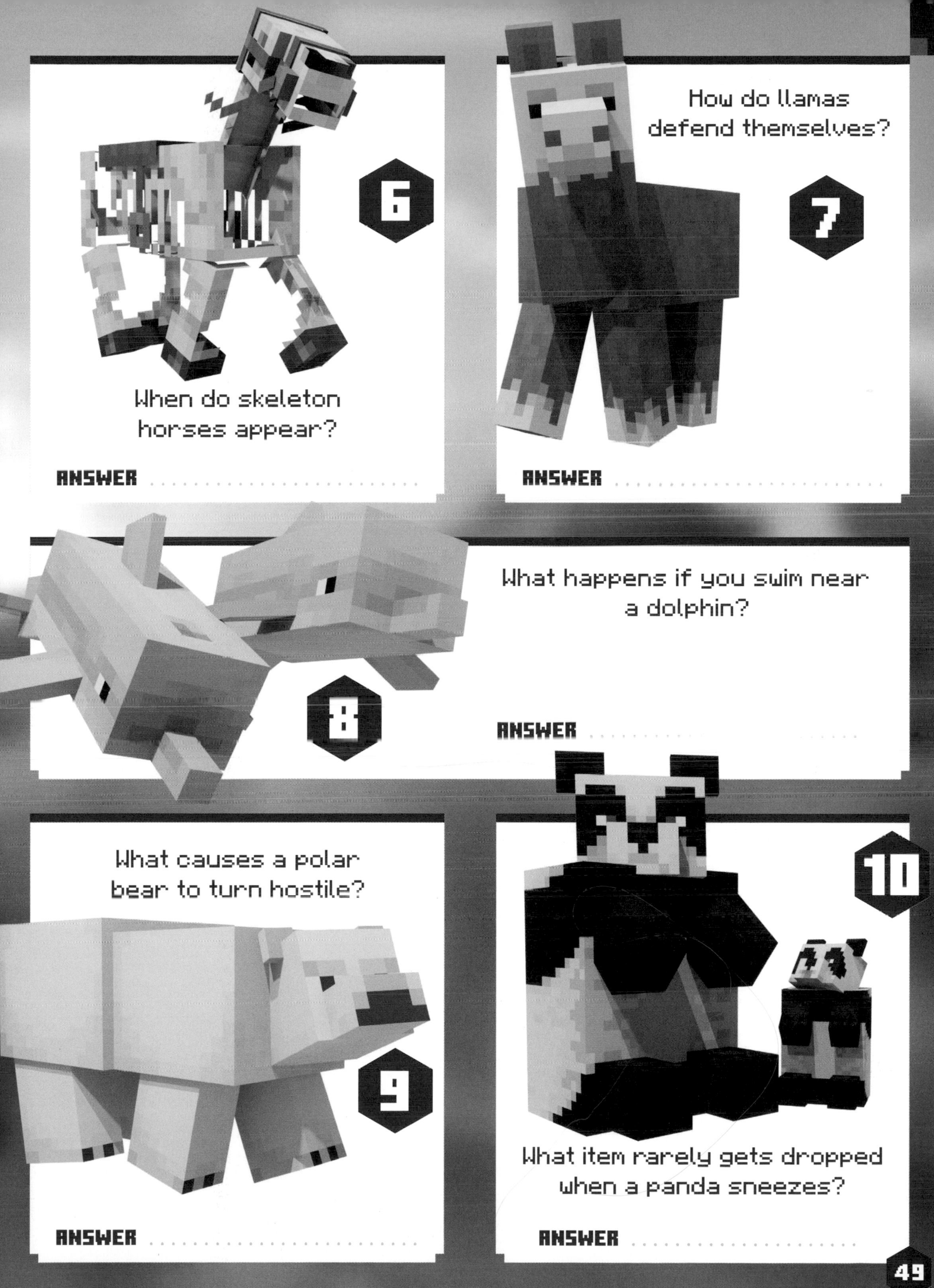

6

When do skeleton horses appear?

ANSWER ....

7

How do llamas defend themselves?

ANSWER ....

8

What happens if you swim near a dolphin?

ANSWER ....

9

What causes a polar bear to turn hostile?

ANSWER ....

10

What item rarely gets dropped when a panda sneezes?

ANSWER ....

Check your answers on page 68

DUNGEONS: SEASONAL ADVENTURES

Swashbuckling heroes had better buckle up! Now that the Vengeful Heart of Ender has been defeated and the Orb of Dominance is destroyed for good, it's time for our dungeon-crawling heroes to set out on their next escapade: seasonal adventures.

SEASONAL ADVENTURES

Seasonal adventures are a new way to progress through the ranks and unlock new rewards. Players can strike out on a new adventure up the Tower to see how far they can survive. Each season brings a new adventure, but don't worry if you miss a season as they'll always be available for you to complete again and again.

THE TOWER

The Tower is a new 30-floor arena in the camp where you can fight mobs and bosses, and meet new Tower inhabitants. Every time you enter the tower, you will start as a fresh character to see how far you can advance. The Tower changes every two weeks to put your exploration and battle skills to the test. The more floors you climb, the greater the rewards.

MOBS

Watch out for new mobs and dangerous mob wave combinations! The new tower wraiths with their special attacks and the tower guards with their deadly melee hits will challenge even the strongest of characters.

NEW REWARDS

Show off to your mates with these awesome new rewards to collect! Compete in daily challenges to earn adventure points and unlock rewards that have not been seen before in the Minecraft universe. Which ones do you want?

CAPES

What superhero doesn't have a cape? Unlock your very own cape and watch as it billows magnificently in the wind.

PETS

Unlock new companions as you complete adventures. There are lots of new pets to unlock, including baby goats, baby turtles and even the adorable baby squid!

SKINS

In case you didn't already have enough skins, there are now even more to choose from to make you look truly awesome and stand out in-game.

EMOTES

Whether you're faceplanting, waving at your mates or busting out some sweet dance moves, there are loads of emotes to collect and impress with your friends with.

FLAIRS

Apply new effects, such as confetti, heart fountains and thunder cracks, to your game and use them to show off when you level up, heal or respawn.

WORDSEARCH

Dungeons are filled with chests hidden in concealed corners and secret levels to be unlocked by eagle-eyed explorers. Can you find all these words hidden in the wordsearch?

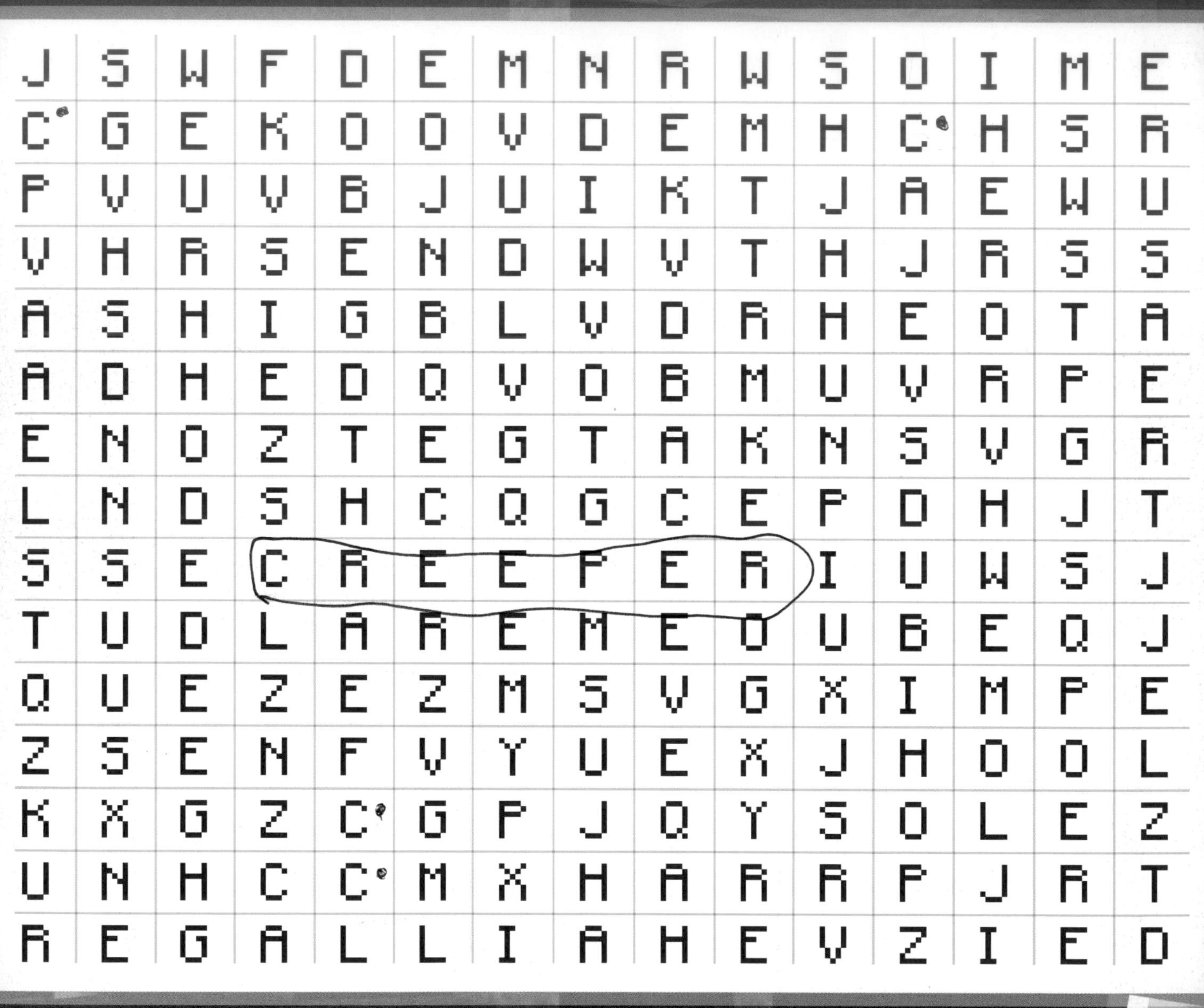

J	S	W	F	D	E	M	N	R	W	S	O	I	M	E
C	G	E	K	O	O	V	D	E	M	H	C	H	S	R
P	V	U	V	B	J	U	I	K	T	J	A	E	W	U
V	H	R	S	E	N	D	W	V	T	H	J	R	S	S
A	S	H	I	G	B	L	V	D	R	H	E	O	T	A
A	D	H	E	D	Q	V	O	B	M	U	V	R	P	E
E	N	O	Z	T	E	G	T	A	K	N	S	V	G	R
L	N	D	S	H	C	Q	G	C	E	P	D	H	J	T
S	S	E	C	R	E	E	P	E	R	I	U	W	S	J
T	U	D	L	A	R	E	M	E	O	U	B	E	Q	J
Q	U	E	Z	E	Z	M	S	V	G	X	I	M	P	E
Z	S	E	N	F	V	Y	U	E	X	J	H	O	O	L
K	X	G	Z	C	G	P	J	Q	Y	S	O	L	E	Z
U	N	H	C	C	M	X	H	A	R	R	P	J	R	T
R	E	G	A	L	L	I	A	H	E	V	Z	I	E	D

WORDS TO FIND

- CREEPER
- EMERALD
- ILLAGER
- NETHER
- SURVIVE
- DUNGEONS
- HERO
- MOBS
- QUEST
- TREASURE
- ZOMBIE

CHALLENGE

SUDOKU

Well done! You've managed to find nine chests full of items. Now you must evenly distribute your treasure between each chest by solving this sudoku. Make sure that no boxes or lines have duplicate items in them!

KEY **If you don't want to draw the items, use the numbers in this key instead.**

1 2 3 4 5 6 7 8 9

Check your answers on page 68

MINECRAFT IN SCHOOL

We all love playing games! They're fun, exciting and keep us engaged for hours. And when we're engaged, we're in the best position to learn. Minecraft: Education Edition recognises this and has created games to teach players new skills. This process is known as gamification and it's the newest, trendiest way to have fun while learning. Let's check out some of the games you can play!

WHY USE MINECRAFT EDUCATION?

Not everyone learns best in a classroom environment. With so many distractions around the classroom and at home, it's no wonder teachers are looking for new ways to capture your attention. Minecraft Education is a great way for you to learn all your lessons but in a fun, creative way. How cool would it be to play Minecraft at school?

FEATURED LESSONS

MUSEUM HEIST

Want to solve a heist, work with Wonder Woman AND learn coding at the same time? We sure did! There has been a robbery at the museum and a priceless painting has gone missing. Help Wonder Woman find out who did it by using basic coding skills and game-design concepts as you navigate the museum, solving puzzles and searching for clues. We love how fun this makes learning coding.

FAIRY TALE REIMAGINED

Have you ever wanted to create your very own fairy tale? Well, here's your chance! We think you'll adore this introduction to digital storytelling as it allows you to be really creative with it. There are a series of activities for you to complete, which will get you reimagining your favourite fairy tales and coming up with new ways to tell them in Minecraft, creating an immersive story experience.

LEARNING WITH MINECRAFT EDUCATION

Minecraft: Education Edition is a game-based learning platform for schools – because what lesson can't be improved with a bit of Minecraft?! There are over 500 lessons, immersive worlds and challenges available for free across a huge range of subjects. It's full of unique blocks and has loads of tools to make learning more fun for both you and your teachers! Maybe you've even used it already.

Jump straight into your first fun-filled learning experience with one of these featured lessons:

RENEWABLE ENERGY

You might not associate renewable energy with fun, but that's exactly why this lesson is so amazing! Find out all about alternative energy sources in an enjoyable, interactive way. You'll be an eco-warrior before you know it!

FRACTIONS

Let's face it, not everyone is a maths whizz, but with this series of mini-games, you just might be by the end of them! We love how this lesson shows fractions in a visual way to help us all understand them easier.

PIXEL SELFIES

Did you know that digital photos are composed of thousands and thousands of square pixels? Use Minecraft blocks as pixels to create a pixel-art drawing of yourself to show your mates and maybe even hang on the wall!

COAT OF ARMS

We love to combine lessons where we can – they're much more fun that way! Here, you get to learn about the history of coats of arms at the same time as getting arty and creating your very own. What will you put on yours?

ICE RACETRACK BUILD CHALLENGE

Looking for a new game to play with your friends? Build an ice boat racetrack to see who's the fastest paddler among you. This racecourse features sharp corners, rough terrain and hazardous zones to test the mettle and skill of all players. Check out page 59 for a detailed diagram on exactly how to make this course.

1 ICE TRACK

Build a racetrack using blue ice. Blue ice will allow you to race quickly down the track, rewarding good steering and punishing bad turns. Avoid bumping into other players – it'll slow you both down!

2 COARSE BLOCKS

Add some snow layers among the blue ice. To get the fastest time, you'll need to weave between these blocks to stay on the blue ice and maintain your speed.

3 HAZARD ZONES

Use powdered snow to create hazardous zones. Crashing into these can make players spin out, or worse, get stuck in the rough!

5 SEATING

Build some seating for the spectators! You can also place item frames with spyglasses around the sides. Spectators can use these to keep a close eye on the action at all times.

4 SHARP CORNERS

Curve the course with some sharp twists and turns to make it more difficult for your players. This will put them through the ultimate steering test!

ICE RACETRACK BUILD CHALLENGE

PART 2

BUNTING

Put up some bunting to show players how far the finish line is by hanging banners from chains. Use a loom to give the bunting some fun and quirky designs.

WINNER!

Find out exactly when a player crosses the finishing line with some redstone lamps! Place a tripwire along the finish line to trigger redstone lamps as soon as a player completes the race.

THE RACING RINK

1.0 HRS MEDIUM

A racetrack that twists and turns will give your racers a real challenge! Build your track with these sharp turns, but don't make them too sharp or you'll be crashing into the walls!

BUILD TIP

Place a barrier around the racetrack to stop players from going off-course – or worse, skipping a section!

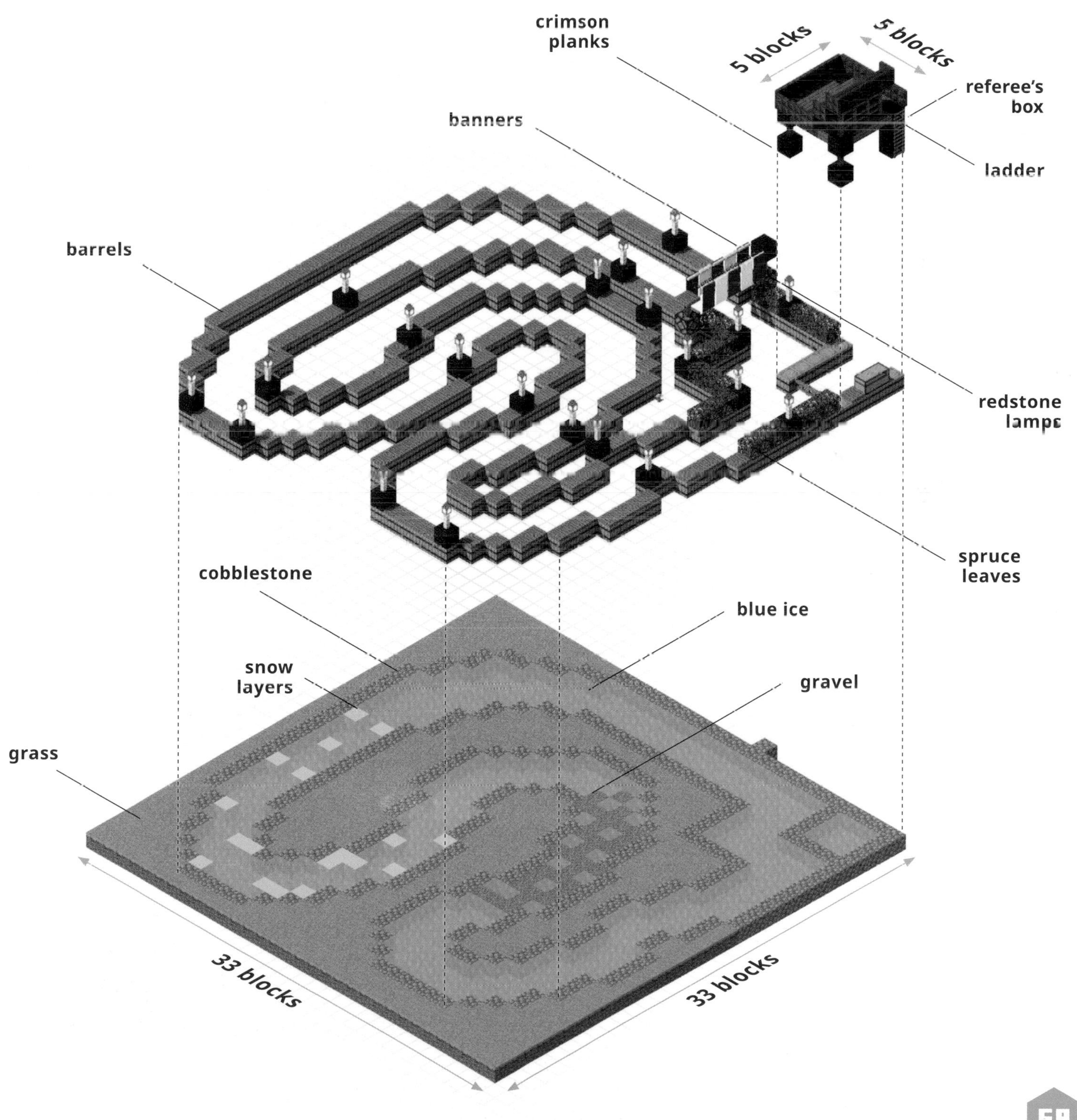

THE WILD UPDATE

This year saw the release of Minecraft's latest update: The Wild Update! This exciting new addition is full of scary adventures and wonderful nature, creating an atmosphere that is both chilling and beautiful. As with any Minecraft update, this one comes with a whole host of new blocks, mobs, biomes, plants, items and many more. Let's explore some of our favourite new additions!

DEEP DARK

Home to the warden, the deep dark biome is set at the deepest depths of the Overworld. This may well be the rarest cave biome in the game and tends to generate under continental/mountainous areas. Explore this biome at your own risk – it is full of sculk shriekers waiting to summon a warden if you accidentally trigger them. However, if you manage to reach the ancient cities within the depths alive, you will be rewarded with chests full of valuable loot – not to mention these deserted cities are truly awesome to explore!

WARDEN

The warden is a giant, terrifying mob that you do not want to cross! They are completely blind, but do not let this fool you into a false sense of security – this mob has wicked hearing and a keen sense of smell. You do not want to make one of these angry – with more health than both the Wither and Ender Dragon, and the hardest hit of any mob, this is the toughest mob out there. Our best advice is to sneak away and hide until it goes away.

FROGS

Naturally spawning in all swamp biomes, frogs can now be found in the Wild Update. These mobs begin their life as tadpoles, which can be gathered in buckets and taken to other biomes, where they will grow up into different kinds of frogs: tan brown if raised in a temperate biome, white in a warm biome, and green in a cold biome. This means that frogs raised in mangrove swamps will be white, while frogs in the normal swamps will grow up to be green.

Once fully grown, a frog will feast on slimes, which it catches using its tongue. You can also feed them slimeballs to breed them. If a frog eats a small magma cube, it will drop a froglight, which can be different colours depending on what colour frog ate it. Cool, right?! What colour frog will you grow first?

SWAMPS

There's a new swamp in Minecraft: the mangrove swamp biome, which is full of – you guessed it – mangroves! Mangroves are the one tree that will generate in this new swamp, and are identified by their large, exposed roots – they're also the only plant in Minecraft that can be planted below water! Mud blocks have also been added to swamps, which you can also create by pouring water on a dirt block.

ALLAY

The people have spoken! The allay has been added to the game by popular vote. With its short body, big white eyes and large wings, this mob is sure to become a fast favourite in-game. Not only are they cute to look at, the allay is also a very useful mob to have around and will collect items for you. You can find them near pillager outposts in dark oak cages or inside jail cells within woodland mansions.

An allay has just one slot in its inventory, but it can stack up to 64 items at once – a lot for such a small creature! Just give it an item, and it will go off in search of others of the same item nearby and collect them for you – useful if you're searching for something in particular and can't find it anywhere.

CHALLENGE

CROSSWORD

Have you been reading closely? See how many words on this crossword you can fill in without searching for the answers, then go on a hunt to find the rest!

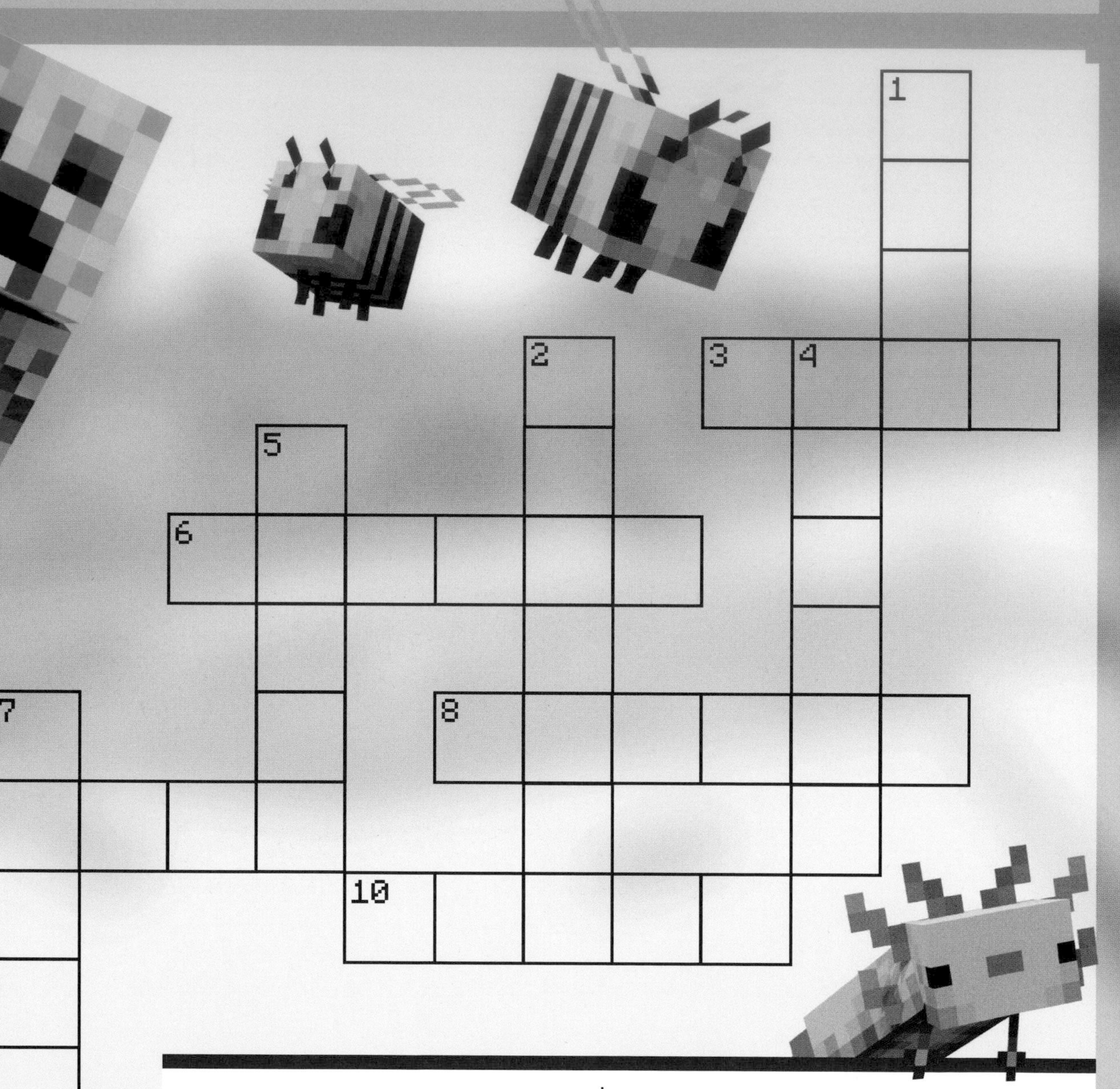

DOWN

1. On page 56, what type of ice is used for the racetrack?

2. On page 24, which mob is mac's favourite?

4. On page 51, what will get your characters dancing?

5. On page 33, what colour were the Endermen's eyes originally?

7. How many swords are on the cover?

ACROSS

3. On pages 26 and 27, what is the most popular mob?

6. On page 29, which gametype has you making your way up through the ranks?

8. On page 9, what new ore has been introduced to the game?

9. On page 40, what is the name of the middle command block?

10. On page 10, which cute creature won the mob vote?

Check your answers on page 68

MINECRAFT
WELCOME TO MY LILY PAD
CUT ALONG DOTTED LINE

MINECRAFT
DUNGEONS
CUT ALONG DOTTED LINE

HOW TO DRAW

It's time to put your artistic skills to the test! These incredibly cute mobs have been spotted roaming the Overworld and are begging to have their portraits drawn. Using the grids as your guide, concentrate on drawing one square at a time until you've completed the pictures. Once you have the outlines, you can go in with your colouring pencils to finish them off!

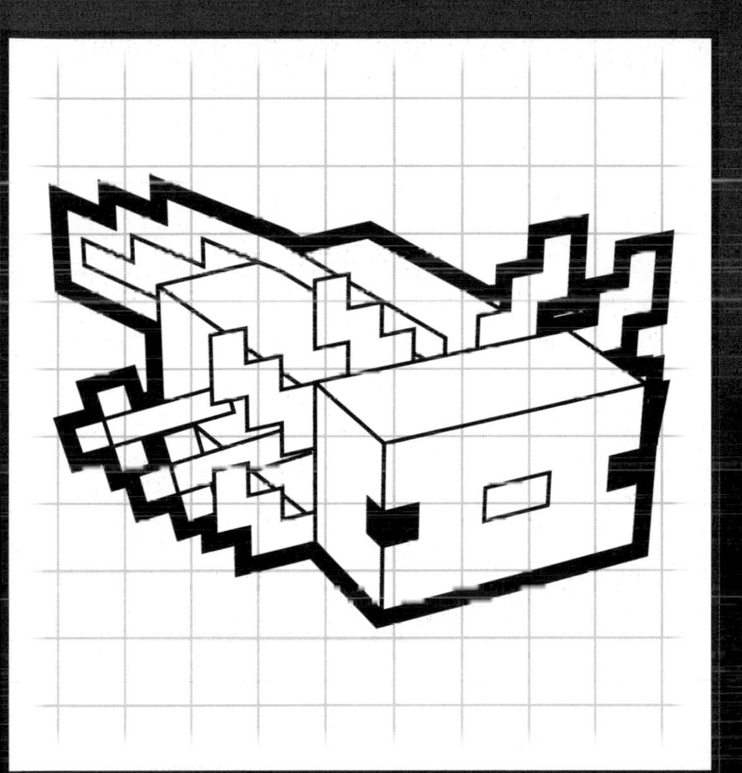

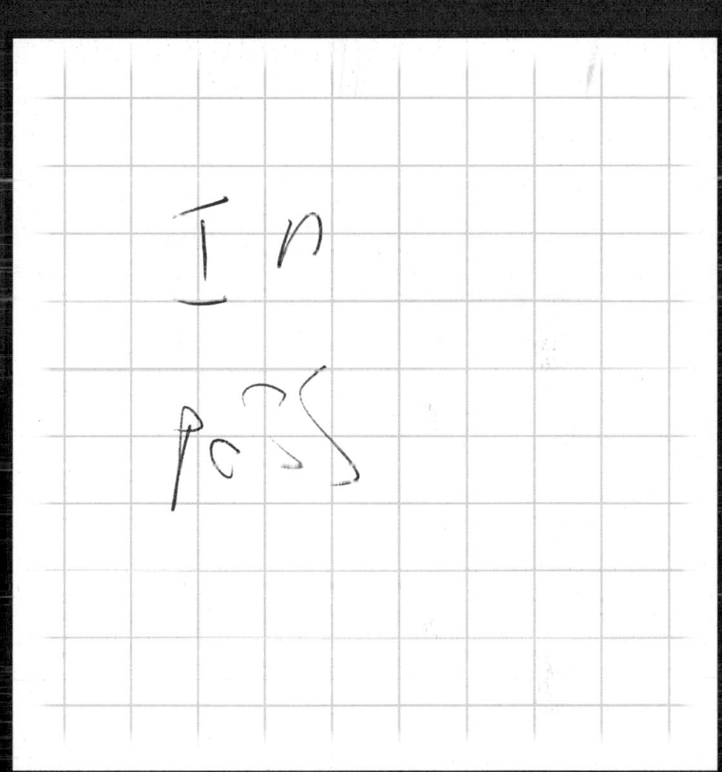

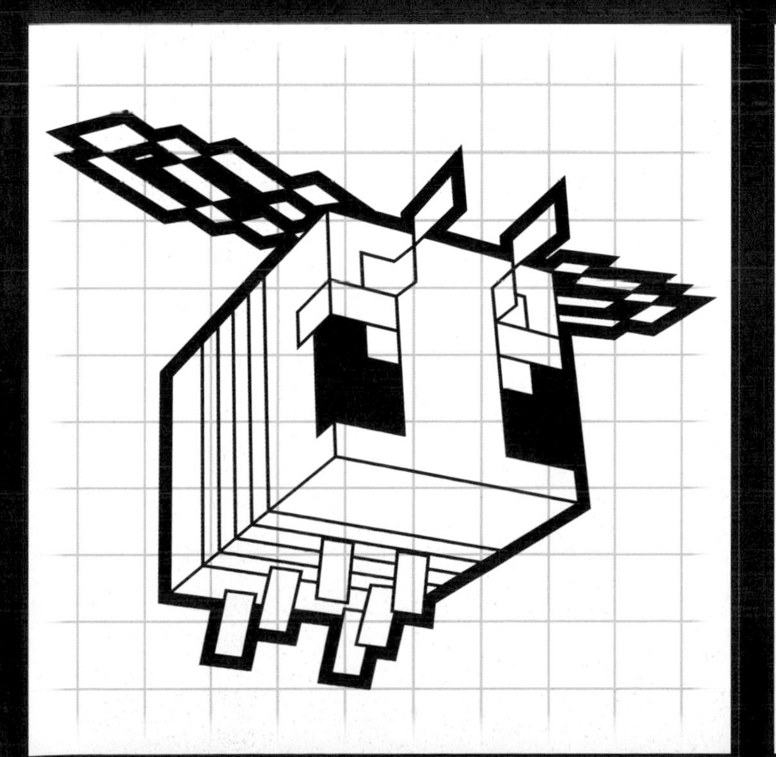

CAMPFIRE TALES

EXPERT GUIDE WITH SPARKS

It has been another amazing year in Minecraft with lots and lots of awesome stories continuing to emerge right from the heart of the game – the community! You have all been so busy making incredible new builds that it's hard to pick our favourites. Let's take a look at some of the awesome things you have done.

GOLDMINE

Over the years, players have found creative ways to create automatic farms for almost every resource in game, be it crops, farm animals, fish or ore. One enterprising player, Spanish Youtuber EIRichMC, has succeeded in making the world's largest Survival mode gold farm. Seven years in the making, and over 600,000 blocks later, the farm yields an astonishing 1,000 gold blocks per hour without the player so much as glancing at a pickaxe!

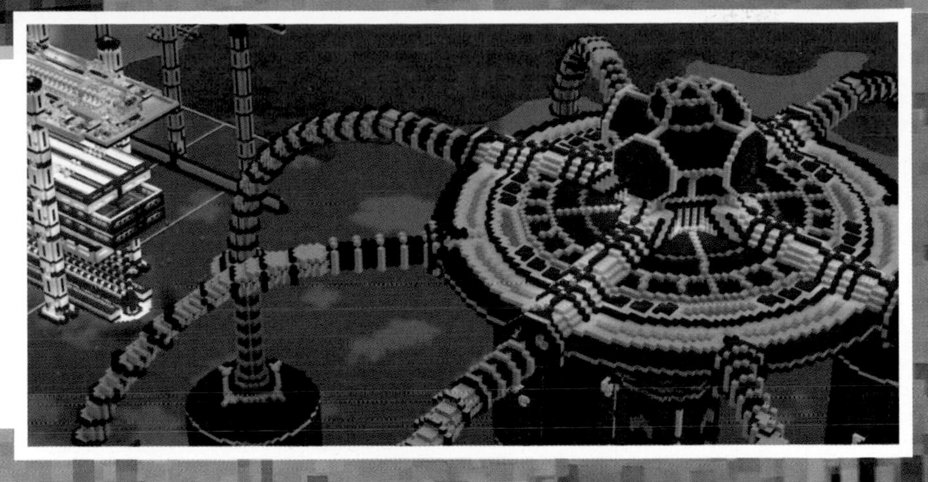

BY - SONJA

BY - VOOV

BI-MONTHLY BUILD CHALLENGE

For the past year, the community has engaged in bi-monthly build challenges on the official Minecraft Discord. Players are given a theme to go away and interpret as they'd like, building an impressive structure in Minecraft, and then submitting their creations to the competition. Themes have included Pirate Cave, Fantasy Book, Revamped Pillager Tower, Land of the Plants, Garden: Back to the Roots and Abandoned Arctic Outpost.

The turnout has been astonishing, with tons of truly impressive builds – too many to pick one favourite. The top three submissions for each challenge are shared online for all feast their eyes on. If you're seeking something new to build and are struggling to come up with what to do next, then these challenges are the perfect place for you to find inspiration.

BY - TOTACOBELL

BY - SANDER

BY - SANDER

BY - CHOMCHOM

ANSWERS

18-19

38-39

1 - F
4 - E
2 - B
5 - C
3 - D
6 - A

48-49

1 - A PURPLE SHEEP
2 - A SCUTE
3 - PLACE A CAMPFIRE UNDER THEIR HIVE
4 - WHEAT
5 - UNDERWATER NEAR CLAY BLOCKS
6 - WHEN LIGHTNING STRIKES
7 - THEY SPIT
8 - YOU GET A SPEED BOOST
9 - IF YOU THREATEN ITS CUBS
10 - A SLIMEBALL

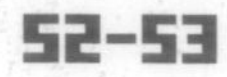

52-53

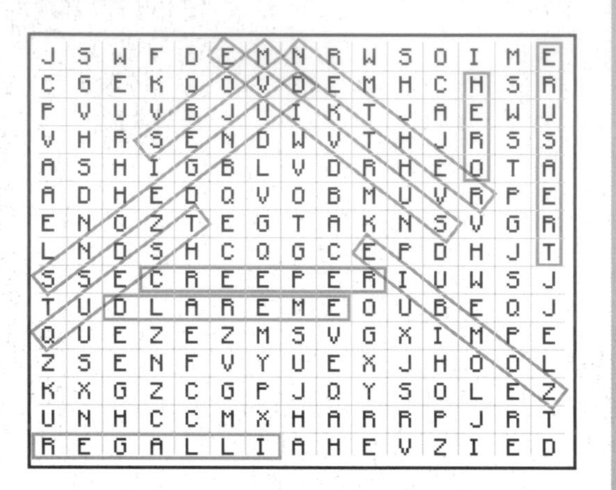

J	S	W	F	D	E	M	N	R	W	S	O	I	M	E
C	G	E	K	Q	O	V	D	E	M	H	C	H	S	R
P	V	U	V	B	J	U	I	K	T	J	A	E	W	U
V	H	R	S	E	N	D	W	V	T	H	J	R	S	S
A	S	H	I	G	B	L	V	D	R	H	E	O	T	A
A	D	H	E	D	Q	V	O	B	M	U	V	R	P	E
E	N	O	Z	T	E	G	T	A	K	N	S	V	G	R
L	N	D	S	H	C	Q	G	C	E	P	D	H	J	T
S	S	E	C	R	E	E	P	E	R	I	U	W	S	J
T	U	D	L	A	R	E	M	E	O	U	B	E	Q	J
Q	U	E	Z	E	Z	M	S	V	G	X	I	M	P	E
Z	S	E	N	F	V	Y	U	E	X	J	H	O	O	L
K	X	G	Z	C	G	P	J	Q	Y	S	O	L	E	Z
U	N	H	C	C	M	X	H	A	R	R	P	J	R	T
R	E	G	A	L	L	I	A	H	E	V	Z	I	E	D

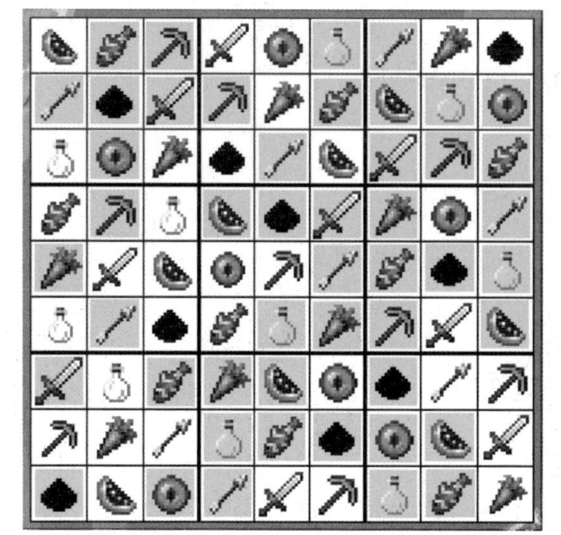

62

DOWN	ACROSS
1 - BLUE	3 - BEES
2 - AXOLOTL	6 - PRISON
4 - EMOTES	8 - COPPER
5 - GREEN	9 - CHAIN
7 - THREE	10 - ALLAY

GOODBYE

That's a lot of Minecraft we've just gotten through! You know what, it feels like we're working together to build a better world. And there's lots more to come next year. Are you ready? Let's go!

Thanks for playing!

Alex Wiltshire
Mojang Studios